For Scout

SIMON & SCHUSTER BOOKS FOR YOUNG READERS
An imprint of Simon & Schuster Children's Publishing Division
1230 Avenue of the Americas, New York, New York 10020

Book design by Lucy Ruth Cummins
The text for this book is set in Letterpress.
The illustrations for this book are rendered in watercolor.
Manufactured in China
10 9 8 7 6 5 4 3 2 1
Library of Congress Cataloging-in-Publication Data
Prosek, James.
Bird, butterfly, eel / story and paintings by James Prosek.—1st ed.
p. cm.
Summary: Follows a bird, a monarch butterfly, and an eel from summer
on a farm until they make their respective fall voyages south, and then
later begin to return north again when the weather warms.
ISBN-13: 978-0-689-86829-0
ISBN-10: 0-689-86829-4
1. Monarch butterfly—Migration—Juvenile fiction. 2. Butterflies—Migration—Juvenile fiction.
3. Birds—Migration-Juvenile fiction. 4. Eels—Migration—Juvenile fiction. [1. Monarch butterfly—
Migration—Fiction. 2. Butterflies—Migration—Fiction. 3. Birds—Migration—Fiction. 4. Eels—
Migration—Fiction.] I. Title.
PZ10.3.P9276Bi 2009
[E]—dc22
2007015734

Bird, Butterfly, Eel

Story and paintings by James Prosek

Simon & Schuster Books for Young Readers

New York London Toronto Sydney

It's summer on the farm, and Bird, Butterfly, and Eel are at home.

Butterfly is a monarch.

She lives in the meadow behind the pond.

Eel lives in the dark, cool waters of the pond, below the lilies.

Bird lives in the barn at the end of the meadow, in nests she made of mud and straw. She loves being safe, high up in the rafters, away from the barn cats.

Butterfly is laying her eggs on the milkweed plants in the meadow.

Soon the eggs hatch
and become caterpillars.
They eat the milkweed
and get strong enough
to spin chrysalises and
become butterflies.

Eel has lived in the pond for many years.

She is eating insects and small fish and storing up energy for her long swimming journey ahead.

Bird flies over the meadow, collecting insects to feed to her babies in the barn.

As summer turns into fall, Bird's young have left the nest and are flying over the pond and meadow, singing songs for Butterfly and Eel. Butterfly watches her young caterpillars turn into beautiful butterflies. Eel is full and strong and is ready for her long journey.

With the cool winds of autumn, Bird, Butterfly, and Eel sense a change, feel restless, and know this means it is time to leave the farm.

Bird gathers her babies and flies southwest over the barn, the meadow, the pond, and follows the coast. Butterfly takes to the southerly winds, heading down over land and sea. Eel swims downstream and out to the ocean.

At one point in their long journey, at the edge of the sea, Bird, Butterfly, and Eel will meet one last time to say good-bye. There they see other animals on their own long journeys to very different places.

Then all of the creatures—striped bass, false albacore, common tern, bay anchovy, osprey, fishermen—go their separate ways. . . .

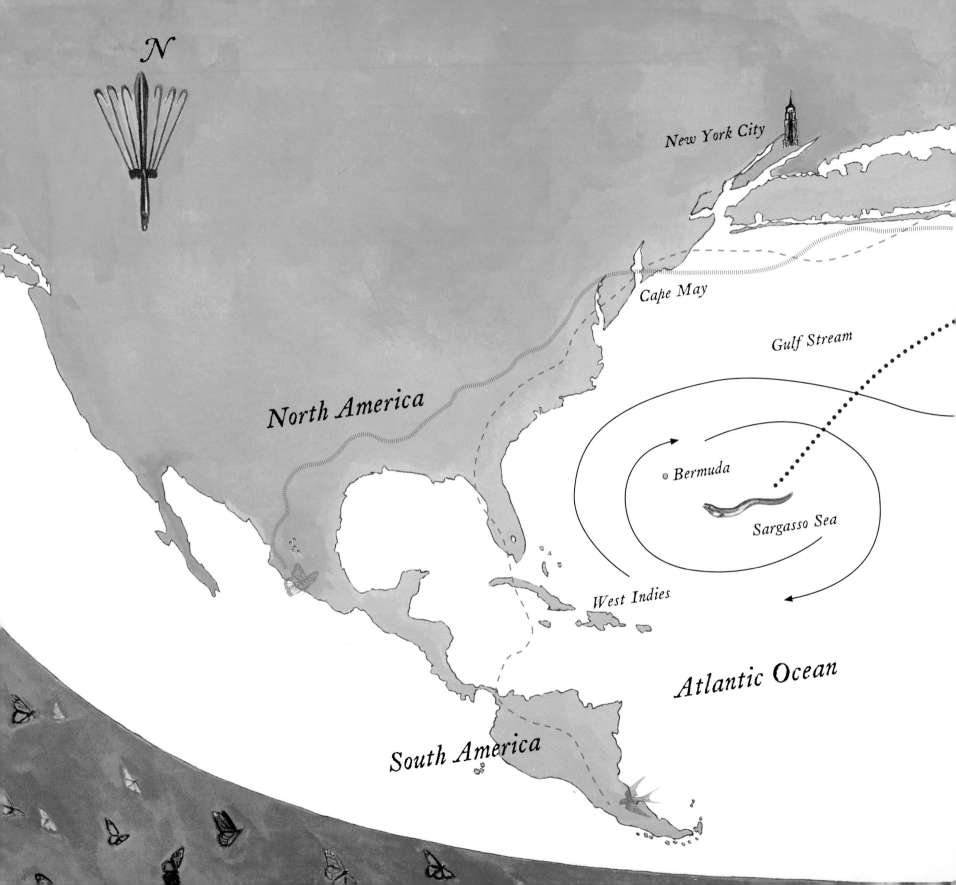

N

New York City

Cape May

Gulf Stream

North America

Bermuda

Sargasso Sea

West Indies

Atlantic Ocean

South America

Farm

Cape Cod

Long Island Sound

Martha's
Vineyard

Long Island

Montauk Point

Bird will go eight thousand miles to the southern tip of Argentina to spend the winter in the golden meadows of Patagonia, which look very similar to the ones she left on the farm.

Butterfly will glide to the mountains of Central Mexico, three thousand miles away, and spend the winter in forests with millions of other butterflies. There are so many butterflies, they blanket the trees.

Eel will swim down the creek connecting the pond to the sea. From the coast she'll travel fifteen hundred miles to the Sargasso Sea, an eddy in the middle of the Atlantic Ocean.

It is warm and beautiful where Bird, Butterfly, and Eel go.

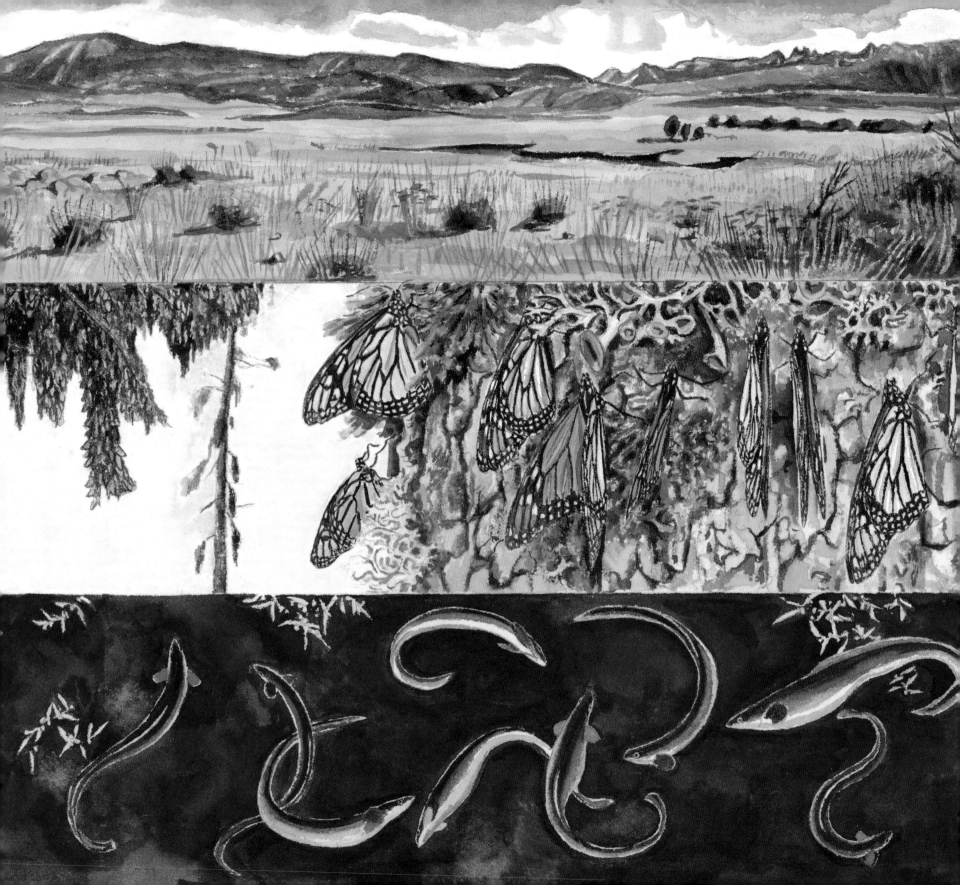

Back on the farm, the barn and the meadow are covered in snow, and the pond begins to freeze. It is cold, and the animals that live there miss Bird, Butterfly, and Eel.

As winter turns into spring on the farm, Bird flies home to her nest in the rafters of the barn where she was born . . . Butterfly makes a long journey north again as spring turns into summer, her young taking her place in the meadow as the flowers begin to bloom . . . and Eel's young, small as toothpicks and clear as glass, swim up the creek to the pond.

And the cycle begins again.

REAL FACTS ABOUT
THE BIRD, THE BUTTERFLY, AND THE EEL

Why don't Bird, Butterfly, and Eel stay on the farm?

At some point in their lives, nearly all creatures on earth make a journey from one place to another. Sometimes they travel to find food, sometimes to meet up with other creatures like themselves. This kind of movement, through air, under water, or over land, is called *migration*.

Some birds and fish make short migrations of a few hundred feet, such as from a lake to an inlet stream, and some migrate as far as thousands of miles, from one hemisphere to the other. Even plants have ways of spreading their seeds over long distances. Some plants have a method of locomotion that acts like a kind of built-in propeller or parachute so that the seed can be carried by the wind. This is the case with the host plant of the monarch butterfly, the milkweed, the seeds of which are each attached to a silky plume.

Monarch Butterfly

The plant that nurtures the caterpillars of any species of butterfly is called a host plant. The idea for this book grew out of my passion for the host plant of the monarch butterfly, the milkweed—in particular, *Asclepias tuberosa*, commonly known as butterfly weed (the orange-flowered plant you see throughout this book). Adult monarchs will lay their eggs on any of the hundred or so species of milkweed, where the caterpillars hatch, eat the plant, grow, and spin themselves into a jeweled green case called a *chrysalis*. The sap of the milkweed plant is toxic and provides the caterpillars with food that will later protect them from predators who might try to eat them.

Several years ago I transplanted some butterfly weed plants to a sunny spot in my front yard. Soon after, the butterflies

monarch egg on bud of milkweed flower

started to lay their single white eggs on the leaves and flower buds of the plants. (Can you find the monarch egg on the leaf on the left side of p. 14?) I found, through the course of the summer, that dozens of caterpillars had hatched and were feeding on the milkweed. I watched the caterpillars grow rapidly, spin their emerald-green chrysalises, and by late July metamorphose into adult monarch butterflies. Monarch butterflies continued to emerge from my garden through August, September, and into October. I learned that these butterflies fly all the way to Mexico to spend the winter on ten to twelve volcanic mountaintops. One winter I traveled to the central province of Michoacán, Mexico, to see the butterflies, which were clustered by the millions in fir trees.

monarch caterpillar

chrysalis

The last generation of monarchs are born in the northern United States and southern Canada in late summer, and in early fall they migrate three thousand miles south to Mexico by rising on columns of warm air called *thermals* to altitudes of twelve thousand feet, gliding down until they catch the next thermal. The monarchs arrive in Mexico in early November and stay in the cool forests there until about March.

In spring the females mate with the males, the males die, and the females fly north as far as they can go before it is their time to lay their eggs on milkweed plants and die. Generally these butterflies have about three weeks to live once they leave Mexico and make it to southern Texas. The caterpillars of the adults grow and emerge as butterflies and have about three to four weeks to live, spreading north, and laying their eggs before they, too, die. This continues until the last brood of the summer returns to Mexico, four or five generations removed from the ones that spent the previous winter there. One of the most remarkable things about the migration of the monarch butterfly is that the butterflies that fly to Mexico have never been there before.

adult butterfly

Barn Swallows

Barn swallows travel from North America, where they breed, to Central and South America, where they spend the winter. Of the creatures in this book, they travel the farthest, some over ten thousand miles. They are named for their preference of building their mud-and-straw nests in barns. They catch their food, mostly insects, in the air.

barn swallow egg

For a long time, it was not known where the monarch butterfly, the eel, and barn swallows went in the winter. People guessed that the swallows transformed into other creatures, or buried themselves in the mud at the bottom of freshwater ponds. Eventually these myths were dispelled, in part by banding, or tagging (tying a small band around a bird's leg to identify it), which taught us that some birds return in spring to the same nest they'd used the previous year. Later, improved tagging technology allowed us to track the swallows' path to their winter grounds. With this information researchers formed a clearer picture of birds' migration routes. It is thought that birds (and butterflies and eels, too) navigate in part by the earth's magnetic field.

barn swallow chick

adult barn swallow

American Eel

Unlike this book's Bird and Butterfly, who have their babies on the farm, Eel has its young in the ocean. The eel is one of the few fish that spawns in saltwater and spends the rest of its life in freshwater and *estuaries*, where freshwater and saltwater meet. Like the monarch, the eel hatches from an egg into a larva, later transforming into an adult that looks very different (see picture). The big change

eel egg

transparent eel larva

that takes place in the butterfly and eel is called *metamorphosis*.

Eel leaves the farm in September and swims about fifteen hundred miles to the Sargasso Sea, a warm circulating eddy in the middle of the Atlantic Ocean. It is thought that spawning takes place in late winter, and it is assumed that the adult eels die after spawning because no adult eels have ever been seen returning up rivers from the sea. But no one can say for sure, as no humans have ever witnessed an eel spawning in the wild.

glass eel

After several days the eggs hatch into small, transparent, leaf-shaped larvae called *leptocephali*. The baby eels drift and grow in floating sargassum weed and are then carried by ocean currents toward the coast. Over time they metamorphose into a thinner eel-shaped creature, still transparent, called a *glass eel*. Larvae that are born in the Sargasso Sea in winter take about a year to drift and swim to the coast of New England (and the farm in this book), eventually entering freshwater rivers, lakes, and ponds where they will live out their adult lives.

There is much more that we don't know about the lives of Bird, Butterfly, and Eel. The mysteries of life are what keep us asking questions, thinking, and using our imaginations. Many things are threatening the lives of these three creatures, from hydroelectric dams for migrating eels to the cutting of fir trees in Mexico, where the butterflies spend their winters. I hope you will come to love Bird, Butterfly, and Eel as much as I do, and will want to help protect them for future generations of humans to stare at in wonder.

adult eel

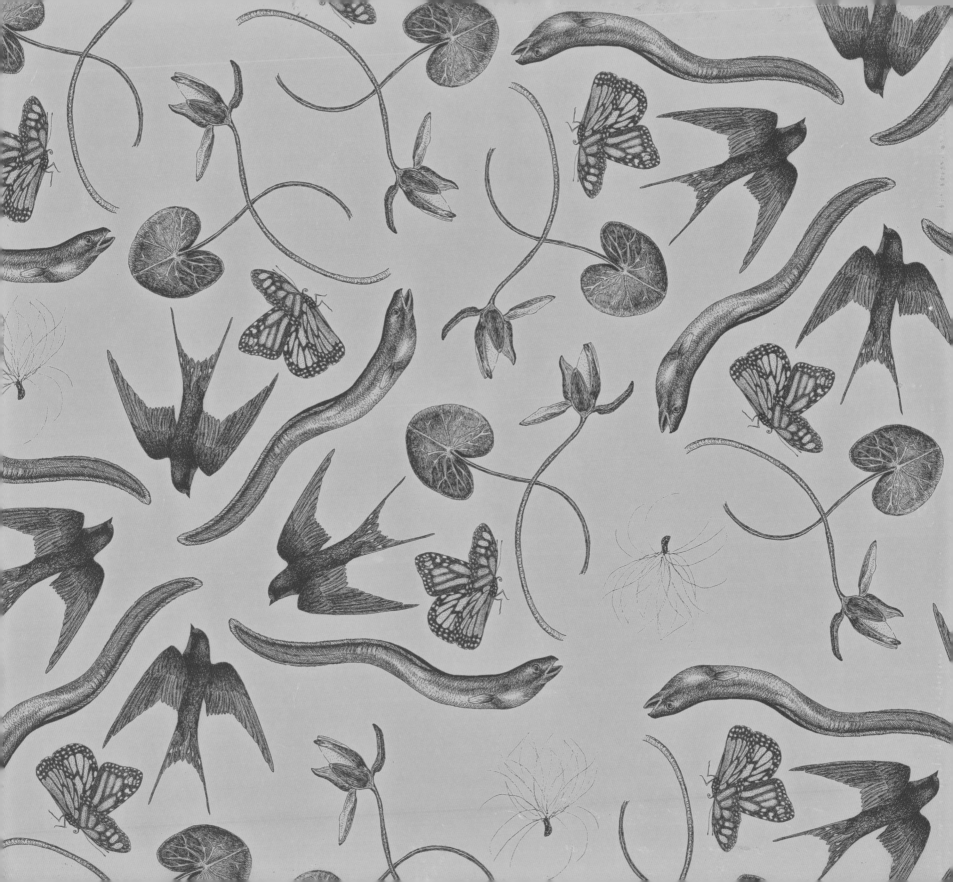